Military

House Hacking

TM

How to Live for Free,
Earn Passive Income and Create
Generational Wealth

Markian Sich - Mike Foster - Eric Upchurch
Adam La Barr - Timothy Kelly - Mitch Durfee

Markian Sich, Michael Foster, Eric Upchurch, Adam La Barr, Timothy Kelly & Mitch Durfee

Copyright © 2018 by Active Duty Passive Income, LLC. All rights reserved. Cover Copyright © 2018 by Active Duty Passive Income, LLC.

No part of this publication may be reproduced or transmitted in any form or by any means, mechanical or electronic, including photocopying and recording, or by any information storage and retrieval system, without permission in writing from the authors.

Disclaimer: The advice and strategies contained herein may not be suitable for every situation. This work is marketed and sold with the understanding that the Authors and Publisher are not engaged in rendering legal, accounting or other professional services. Neither the Authors nor the Publisher shall be liable for damages arriving here from. There are no endorsements of organizations, websites or other here within. Readers should be aware that the information provided may have changed between when this work was written and when it is read.

Paperback ISBN: 978-1-729-23251-4
eBook ISBN: 978-0-692-19778-3

Dedication

We would like to dedicate this book to the courageous men and women of the United States Armed Forces – past, present and future. Because of their sacrifices we can embrace liberty, the ability to pursue happiness, and the right to earn financial freedom.

"I serve with the memory and pride of those who have gone before me, for they loved to fight, fought to win, and would rather die than quit." - NSDQ

Contents

Introduction 1

The Test: Is this book right for you? 4

A Quick Exercise: Financial Freedom Number 7

Good Debt and Assets 12

House Hacking: Goodbye Living Expenses! 16

House Hacking Strategies 24

Other Value-add Hacks 45

House Hacking: Real-Life Examples 49

    Tim's Story 49

    Eric's Story 56

    Mike's Story 69

    Adam's Story 76

    Mitch's Story 81

    Interview: Nico Gibbs 89

Never Sell 94

Conclusion 96

Acknowledgements 99

ADPI Resources 100

Foreword

When Markian and his team asked me to write the Foreword for a book that was being written for the sole purpose of becoming a valuable financial resource for members of the U.S. Military, I jumped at the opportunity. I am honored and humbled to speak to the value and importance of this book for members of our esteemed military.

I am traveling in Italy and France as I write this, remembering what our military did to help these countries in World War II and the ultimate sacrifices many of our soldiers gave to keep our world safe from tyrants.

The courageous and valued members of our military are trained to be warriors, but they, like most people in our great country, are not trained to be financially successful. This simple yet very valuable book bridges that gap.

My name is Rod Khleif and I have owned over 2,000 homes and apartments buildings so far in my real estate investing career. I'm the host of the number one multifamily real estate podcast in the world, "Lifetime Cash Flow through Multifamily Properties" which at the time of this writing has been downloaded over four million times. I am also the author of the book, "How to Create Lifetime Cash Flow through Real Estate

Investing." I say this only to lend credibility to my next statement.

If you are presently in the military, or have been in the past, and you know you want and deserve more financial freedom for yourself and your family, then you must read this book and connect with the Active Duty Passive Income team and community.

You must learn how to utilize the incredible lending opportunities our government has provided to our military. The VA Loan program was established to help our military members become homeowners but can also be utilized to help you create financial freedom for yourself and your family. And that is only one of the many tools explained within these pages.

Study this book, connect with this team and push through any financial fear that you must take massive action with what you learn here.

You deserve it.

With deep, sincere gratitude,

Rod Khleif

Introduction

House Hacking - an investment method in which you can become a homeowner, a real estate investor and a landlord all in one small, and very accessible deal. By implementing strategic investment principles with your primary residence, you can reduce or eliminate living expenses altogether.

More specifically, *military* house hacking, is when those who have served our country in the Armed Forces incorporate some of their unique benefits and strategies which can accelerate their investment success.

This Book is Not for Everyone

Let us get one thing straight: I love the Marine Corps, The United States of America, and everything that this country has provided for my family. My government paycheck is more than enough to cover my living expenses, and we even get to take some great vacations on our own dime. However, since I discovered real estate investing a few years ago, I've been on an unstoppable, steady track to break the military's financial mindset.

This book serves as an important introduction to that mission. Because many people are focused on traditional investment strategies, this book will not be suited for everyone. In fact, this book may not be accepted by some military members and veterans. They may avoid it. They may even reject it.

Why? The structured nature of the military is not conducive to the development of an entrepreneurial mindset. Our military has one key focus – to defend our nation at all costs. If service members start getting distracted by earning money elsewhere – following passions that fall outside of their military responsibilities – a part of their daily work ethic and concentration on the mission, could fall to the wayside.

The question I asked myself many years ago was, "Is there a way that military service and entrepreneurship can complement each other?" This thought morphed into, "Is there a way I can actively set myself up for a more comfortable and stress-free transition into the civilian world while still on active duty?" This book explores these questions and answers them.

Before you are done reading this book, you will be convinced that it is not only possible to be a military entrepreneur by investing in real estate, but that if done correctly it can make you even more effective at your military occupation. Not to mention, make you incredibly wealthy, allow you to retire earlier, and open a door to a behind-the-scenes view of our country's financial "engine room."

Military House Hacking is not going to give you all the answers. Its purpose is to introduce thought-provoking concepts, so you can choose to take the next step.

When that time comes, connect with us at www.activedutypassiveincome.com.

The Test: Is this book right for you?

Throughout our military careers we are taught to be winners in battle and in training. We're expected to be "squared away" at home and in all facets of our lives. So, why aren't we taught winning financial strategies as well?

Our military structure demands uniformity to instill discipline and to guarantee measurable results in war. However, like a powerful tornado, military uniformity is a relentless force that sweeps financial wisdom away and drops it in the same time slot as a run-of-the-mill holiday safety brief. Military financial wisdom becomes more of a checklist procedure within a PowerPoint presentation. It is often considered one of the stereotypical "external difficulties" in our military lives that are forced into a box: uniform and simplified.

You can sense the non-entrepreneurial mindset immediately, Day 1, when you check into bootcamp:

"You aren't smart enough and you don't have the time to invest wisely!"

"Put your money away in the TSP and do your job!"

"Don't you dare buy an expensive car outside of base!"

"Don't get a credit card, you will never get out of debt!"

Sound familiar? It's the same old mindset.

Our military suffers from an epidemic of financial illiteracy. Unfortunately, the current education strategy is inadvertently insulting our intelligence and boring ourselves with financial "death-by-PowerPoint." As a result, our service members have been groomed to worry more about saving money than becoming wealthy.

So here is the test. Answer the following questions below:

- Have you ever found yourself brainstorming for a way you could earn another stream of income?

- Have you ever felt like the only financial wisdom you have received is always focused on saving more and more for when you are 65 years of age and ready to retire?

- Have you ever, even for a second, thought about how nice it must be for your landlord when they collect their rent checks from you?

- Have you ever felt a little awkward or restrained when someone insinuates (perhaps not purposefully) that wanting to be wealthy is a bad thing?

If you find yourself answering "Yes" to any of these questions, then reading this book will feel like scratching an insatiable itch. It will quench your thirst for learning how to expand your financial horizons.

It will NOT be an answer to all your questions, but that's the point. This book is meant to create a spark within that will get your gears turning and will make you question patronizing financial advice.

Now let's turn our attention directly to a new mindset and strategy that can pull you out of the rat race and into a life where you can create generational wealth for your family. Let's calculate your Military Financial Freedom Number™.[1]

---

[1] The abbreviated "Financial Freedom Number" term in this book is in reference to the "Military Financial Freedom Number", Trademarked by Active Duty Passive Income, LLC.

A Quick Exercise: Financial Freedom Number

Do you know what your financial freedom number is? If not, this is an exciting way to really understand what your financial goal for retirement should be, instead of just hoping to save some arbitrary amount over $1,000,000 in your IRA or Thrift Savings Plan (TSP). Ultimately, it will help you calculate how many rental properties (or some other asset) you will need to generate enough monthly passive income so that you can retire.

Let's do a quick exercise that will give you a clearly defined picture of what your exact financial goals in retirement should be. But first, I want to ensure you understand what I mean by the word "retirement." When real estate investors say "retirement" we do not typically mean sitting around on a rocking chair on your porch. You will find that the real estate investing crowd sees retirement as a pleasant and rewarding outcome derived from achieving one's financial freedom number. Hence, we use the term "financial freedom" almost synonymously with "retirement."

If you decide to step into the world of real estate investing and become a part of our community, knowing your financial freedom number is crucial. So, let's get yours calculated, written down, and placed in a very visible location. This is not only your goal; this exercise is the first step towards reaching your dreams.

PART 1: Financial Freedom Number Calculation

Step 1: Calculate your last three (3) months of expenses across all your credit cards and bank accounts. You can leave out major unusual expenses, such as a new car or a 90" TV you bought after deployment. Your expenses should include housing expenses (rent or mortgage), car payments, retirement deposits, Internet, phone, utilities, restaurants, groceries, entertainment, etc.

Step 2: Divide your number by three (3) to get the average.

Step 3: Your financial freedom number equals that number multiplied by 1.5 and rounded **UP** to the nearest thousand.

EXAMPLE:

1. Three month's expenses = $13,666.68.
2. Average = ($13,666.68)/3 = $4,555.56.

3. $4,555.56 x 1.5 = $6,833.34.
    a. Financial Freedom Number = **$7,000**

The $7,000 in this example represents how much money would be needed **every month** to achieve financial freedom or "retirement." You multiply the number by 1.5 (or increase it by 50%) simply because you want to be extra conservative and have enough to buy that occasional TV, go on vacation with your family, or feel comfortable knowing you can pay all your bills.

PART 2: Calculate How Many Assets You'll Need

Now it's time to calculate how many rental properties you will need to achieve your financial freedom number. Expenses will vary, but on average your monthly bottom line should be positive. The positive cash that remains after all expenses have been paid is what real estate investors call **cash flow**. Your goal is to purchase enough rental properties, so the combined total of each property's cash flow reaches or surpasses your monthly financial freedom number.

Let's stick to our figure of $7,000 from our previous calculation to keep the numbers easy.

Prior to buying a primary residence at each duty station, you must first scrutinize its income potential. You will run an analysis to ensure it can produce a net-positive income. In the example below, we will say that our minimum cash flow is $250 per month.

In locations where the market simply will not produce a high enough positive cash flow, you can shift your focus to purchasing properties in other markets. These assets may be in the form of Turnkey rental properties, which isn't "hacking", but can be a great asset to add to your portfolio if you have the down payment. You may never live in some of these homes, but real estate investors are okay with this fact. We view our rental properties like mini-businesses, so it's important to be agile.

Let's do the math.

There is only one step in this calculation:

- Financial Freedom Number / average monthly cash flow
- **Our example: $7,000 / $250 = 28 rental properties.**

If your financial freedom number and the subsequent number of properties seems like an unattainable number to you, keep reading. By the end of this book, you will see that purchasing rental properties can become a part of how your family runs its finances. It is a path to financial freedom that has been followed by many service members. Moreover, there are many ways to accelerate the number of properties you own. If you want to see a more thorough explanation of how you can achieve this before you retire from the military, go to: (https://www.youtube.com/watch?v=MvNdUZkfcuM).

Now put this book aside and do your own calculations **right now**. It should not take you more than five minutes. As soon as you calculate your number, go to our Facebook Group (www.militaryrealestateinvesting.com) and post your result!

Good Debt and Assets

Without first understanding an asset versus liability and good versus bad debt, the rest of this book could be useless. For this reason, I want to provide a basic understanding of these two concepts to ensure the rest of the book is as effective as possible. It will serve as the basis for creating the right mindset needed to become successful real estate investor.

A simple definition of the two words is this:

An asset is something that increases your net worth (puts money in your pocket). A liability is something that decreases your net worth (takes money out of your pocket).

For example, a car is almost always a liability. Unless you purchased a muscle car in the 1960s and kept it in a garage for the past 50+ years, I doubt your car is making you any money. Its value is depreciating, *and* you are paying for it every month - that sucks. The only other way that you could consider your vehicle as an asset is if you choose to walk or bike to work and rent your car to someone else.

An example of an asset would be a rental property. A property that has tenants paying off your debt and generates a little extra cash flow every month is an asset. It puts money *in* your pocket after expenses, each month. I would even argue that with real estate investing, a property is not an asset unless it cash flows (produces more money each month than its operational expenses). If my mortgage is $2,000 a month and I am only getting $1,500 in rent every month from the tenant(s), that property is stifling my lifestyle instead of enhancing it. It's a liability rather than an asset.

A viewpoint that could present a problem would be if an owner treats a rental property that does not have a monthly positive cash flow as an asset, simply because of the net gain in equity each month. That may be true, but it is a slippery slope for a real estate investor to think this way. Cash flow should always be viewed as a paycheck. You are trying to create passive income and establish financial security and freedom for your family. Do not ruin the best part of real estate investing by putting your hard-earned money into a property that decreases your cash flow or relies on appreciation. We invest for cash flow only.

Another problem that I see happen often is people start to fear debt so much that they aim to pay it off as quickly as possible. This is NOT always the best solution.

To explain why, here is my personal definition of "good" and "bad" debt:

Good debt is debt that enables you to purchase an ASSET.

Bad debt is debt on a LIABILITY.

In other words, good debt *makes* you more money than it *costs* you every month. Bad debt is simply taking money away from you.

You should get excited about good debt and shy away from bad debt. Sometimes, however, our lifestyle requires us to accept bad debt, like that car purchase we just mentioned. This is where many people fall into another peculiar mindset trap and act emotionally.

If you have bad debt that is a *very* low interest rate, it may not be the best strategy to pay it off early! Why? Because you should make that money work for you: turn it into an asset. Do not throw that extra cash - potential working-capital - towards something that is already a liability.

For example, if you buy a car that puts you $20,000 in debt, at a 4% interest rate it will cost you roughly $361 a month to pay it off over a five-year period. That comes out to about $1,660 total in interest. What if instead of paying cash for that $20,000 car (because you have an emotional aversion to purchasing depreciating liabilities now), you invested it into an asset that earned you 8% interest annually?

You would instead *profit* by $1,660 after just the first year of investing that same $20,000! Moreover, now you have the remaining four years to pocket that extra income and determine your next investing opportunity. Or if having that extra car ever becomes a necessity, you have now increased your net worth; your ability to afford it.

Investing in real estate, as will be discussed in depth throughout this book, can yield even higher returns – in perpetuity!

House Hacking: Goodbye Living Expenses!

As was defined earlier, the intent behind house hacking is to reduce or eliminate living expenses altogether. If you are flexible and creative, you might even make a net profit each month. By incorporating your unique military benefits and by following some basic methods outlined in this book, you can become very successful. It is not required that you still be active duty to house hack either. Later, you will learn about some common civilian practices, as well as out-of-the-box strategies our team has implemented – even after military service.

As I alluded to previously, I am not going to discuss how to save a dollar here and there by eliminating life's simple and, sometimes necessary, pleasures. The purpose of this book is not to explain frugality or all the things you shouldn't be doing. I would much rather discuss ways to improve your day-to-day lifestyle by eliminating your biggest expense, and explaining how to invest your newly-liberated money into assets that will increase your income.

Before we get into specific strategies of house hacking, let us identify your biggest expense each month. The cost of housing. Since our focus is going to be on reaching your financial freedom number as rapidly as possible, you should start shifting your mindset from saving money, to investing it. If you can eliminate your largest expense, you can invest that money, instead, into income-producing assets.

Rental properties, for instance, are an asset class that can cash flow very well and have multiple ancillary benefits (taxes, appreciation, loan reduction, leverage, hedge against inflation, etc.). If you compound the cash flow and other perks from owning multiple properties over time, things start to get exciting.

Unless you live very inexpensively, or someone is being kind and letting you live with them for free, I am willing to bet that your housing cost is higher than any of your other revolving, monthly expenses. Think about that for a second. Many people learn to simply accept these expenses as an inevitability.

Let's use my life as an example. My wife and I enjoy going out to dinner frequently. But that cost is still no comparison – our housing expenses still far exceed our restaurant and other leisure expenses combined. This is an important point to make because many people have a strange rationale when trying to save money. People I know try crazy things like switching to a Ramen-only lunch diet. They do this just to save $50 every week. I guess I cannot blame them too much; learning to be frugal – an extreme "Saver" – is being taught rampantly in the U.S. Even I had this mindset at one point. I slept on a futon for two years, so I could afford to travel to France to see my girlfriend (who's now my wife).

A Saver's Mindset:

- Save money on small everyday pleasures and put that extra cash into a retirement fund.
- Constantly worry about how much your debt is costing over time.
- Every time new expenses arise in your life (like children), you find yourself painfully cutting out more of life's pleasures and saving more to help pay for expenses in the future (like college tuition).
- Compare prices on nearly everything.

If you were brought up to have a Saver mindset as most Americans are, you may have found yourself thinking about how big of an impact that $50 would make over time. Let's flip the table and execute a truly impactful strategy of investing instead of trying to painfully reduce our everyday pleasures.

An Investor's Mindset:

- Cut out your biggest expenses and invest that difference into assets that produce cash flow.
- Take that newly-produced cash flow and incrementally invest it into more cash-producing assets.
- Save money for the sole purpose of *investing*.
- Love debt that costs little and is used to purchase high-yielding assets.

With this in mind, challenge yourself to do three things to shift from a Saver mindset to an Investor mindset:

- Create more streams of income (side hustle, real estate, tax returns, work bonuses, etc.).
- Eliminate all your biggest expenses (living expenses) and invest that money in assets that create more income.
- Get obsessed with education on this topic. Abe Lincoln once said, "Give me six hours to chop down a tree and I will

spend the first four sharpening the ax." Sharpen your mind in the same way! The Active Duty Passive Income community is a great place to start!

If nothing else, eliminating your housing expense first will render immediate and impactful results in your monthly lifestyle. More importantly, however, it will allow you to invest that money and *exponentially* increase your income farther down the road.

Once you have made the decision to shift your mindset, you can then begin taking action; implementing strategies that allow you to pursue your freedom number.

There are a dozen ways to house hack, but this book is dedicated to explaining tried and true methods of house hacking for military members, veterans, and their families. Only two-tenths of one percent of the world's population are eligible to take advantage of some of these methods! The strategies here, if pursued aggressively, could accelerate your timeframe in reaching your financial freedom number.

This is what you need to get started for a traditional approach to military house hacking:

- Four to eight years, or one to two duty rotations in the military
- VA Loan eligibility, or some startup capital for an FHA Loan
- A defined strategy every year that would increase the value of your home beyond that of your neighbors
- To never lose sight of the goal

Next, you need to understand how to evaluate a potential investment property. Let us cover the fundamental two-step process that almost all real estate investors use as a baseline analysis when looking for an investment property.

1% Rule

This rule requires the monthly rent for the subject property to be no less than 1% of the purchase price. It serves as a great back-of-the-napkin method to analyze a potential deal, so you can decide quickly whether to pursue it further.

The 1% rule takes two elements of a property into consideration: the purchase price and the potential rent. To see if a house is a worthy rental property, simply divide the potential rent by the purchase price.

Example:
- Potential rent: $1,000

- Purchase Price: $110,000
- 1,000/110,000 = **0.9%**

As you see in this example, this particular property would not meet the 1% rule; the monthly rent is less than 1% of the purchase price. It could still be a great rental, but we would need to take our analysis a step further to really see its full potential. You would have to request more information from the broker/agent, maybe request a tour of the property, get inspections done, receive repair bids from contractors or more.

PITI-PMMV

This is acronym often used to describe the total out-of-pocket monthly expenses for an investment property. Ideally, the rent you collect monthly from the tenant(s) will be greater than the total PITI-PMMV value.

- **P**rincipal - monthly core debt to the bank
- **I**nterest - monthly cost to borrow from the bank
- **T**ax - property tax, often between 1%-2%
- **I**nsurance - property liability insurance
- **P**roperty **M**anagement - a fee typically between 7%-10% of the rent for leasing, managing repairs and upkeep, evictions and more.
- **M**aintenance (repairs) - typically 5%-10%
- **V**acancy - typically 5%-10%

When you find a property that meets the 1% rule, you would then subtract PITI-PMMV from the rent to reveal your monthly cash flow. If the result is a net positive number, you have found a property that is likely a great investment.

To this point, you have been taught what is considered and asset, how to shift your mindset to that of an investor, and how to evaluate a potential deal. Next, we will focus on some of the most commonly applied strategies.

House Hacking Strategies

Single-family VA Loan Hacking

The VA Loan, single-family hack is perfect for those with little to no cash savings. It allows you to buy a decent home where are stationed with a 0% down payment. You can even roll the VA Loan funding fee and closing costs into the loan.

A quick note on the VA Loan funding fee: *the funding fee is waived for veterans with a 10% disability rating or greater. Also, you may be eligible for a full refund of the fee retroactively. If the source of your disability was from an occurrence prior to the closing of your property, you are eligible. Make sure to request a refund when you receive your official disability rating.*[2]

This method is not always perfect for married couples and/or families because the key element to this hack is renting out extra bedrooms to friends, family or comrades. It could be perfect for a group of younger military members who all get Basic Allowance for Housing (BAH) or who would have rented a house or apartment together otherwise. This is a lifestyle

---

[2]https://www.veteransunited.com/education/library/va-funding-fee-refund

decision, so I would recommend you consider your specific situation prior to jumping in to this method.

I would have benefited from using this strategy in flight school. My classmates and I just rented a place because we thought it would be "easier." However, some students bought a relatively new three-bedroom, two-bathroom home in a good location. They were able to rent it to other students while they lived in it. Genius! I wish I had thought of that. Because they rented out two of their three rooms, some found themselves cash-positive every month. They were reaping the benefits back then and are still profiting from these properties many years later. Rents in Pensacola have gone up and mortgage payments remained the same. In fact, loan principal and interest payments (the largest portions of a mortgage payment) will remain the same for the full 30 years of their loan. So, each year, if rents increase by 3% as they have historically, positive cash flow will also increase.

The main idea behind single-family VA Loan hacking:

- Buy a house with more bedrooms than you need (preferably with the 1% rule in mind for long-term investment)
- Lease the other rooms to reduce your out-of-pocket mortgage cost. Ideally, the rent collected pays your full mortgage amount!

Here is an example of an aggressive but effective approach to the VA Loan single-family house hacking method. Let's use First Lieutenant (1stLt, O-2) Jones for our example. Here's the breakdown:

- 1stLt Jones checks into his first CH-53E squadron at MCAS New River, NC.
- He purchases a four-bedroom home for approximately $175,000.
- He pays $1,073 (mortgage) + $80 (utilities) every month: $1,153 total.

- He finds three roommates, one for each extra bedroom. They pay him $500 each: $1,500 total.
- 1stLt Jones pays his mortgage with the rental income and is left with $347 each month in cash flow.
- He then takes the $347 and adds it to his $1,044 in monthly BAH for a total of $1,391.

- Jones thinks he can take it one step further to ensure his strategy works out perfectly, so . . .
- Rather than spend the extra money, he puts that $1,391 towards the principal debt every month.
- After twelve months, this totals $16,692. This amount is on top of the $2,758.77 he has paid off the principal simply by paying his mortgage. As a result, 1stLt Jones has paid off $19,450.77 of his loan principal, which is 11.11% of his home's total value!
- At this point, 1stLt Jones knows he can refinance the house with a conventional residential bank loan, which allows him to get his full VA Loan eligibility back!

After refinancing, since Lieutenant Jones only owns 11.11% of his house, he will have to pay a slightly higher interest rate and/or maybe Primary Mortgage Insurance (PMI). This is common unless you have at least an 80% loan-to-value (LTV). This does not bother him because he knows that putting in any additional cash he's saved over the last year would hurt his reserves. Jones, the now real-estate-savvy guy that he is, would rather use that money for rehabbing his next home or save it for another investment that would produce more in monthly income down the road.

1stLt Jones is motivated by his success, keeps the momentum moving and takes the next step. Since he now has his VA Loan eligibility back, he decides to move and purchase a similar house using a similar strategy.

His options are as follows.

Move with the same tenants:

- His tenants (fellow 1stLt's) move with him and maybe he offers to pay for moving them.
- He would then find a good property manager to manage and find new tenants for his first house.
- Now his first property has become an almost completely hands-off, cash flowing rental property.

Leave the tenants in place:

- He leaves his current tenants in his first house.
- A property manager fills his vacancy with a new tenant and provides a new lease with all remaining tenants.
- 1stLt Jones finds new tenants for the new house he will house hack. Again, he can find two or three people he already knows to fill the new house.

1stLt Jones can do this process three more times before he PCS's to his next duty station.

At the end of his four years in North Carolina:

- All four houses start growing his networth by a total of approximately $1,500 every month, and this number slowly increases due to annual rent increases and appreciation.
- He owns about 10-15% equity in four similar houses for a grand total of about $100,000 (that he did not pay for).
- Moreover, he's making about $100-$200 in positive cash flow from every house. 1stLt Jones uses these extra income streams to enhance his comfort of living and lifestyle.

It is clear why this house hacking strategy is the most popular: it's simple.

Small Multifamily Hacking with VA Loan or FHA/203K Loan

This method is perfect for those who already have a family or simply don't want anyone living in their spare bedrooms. It allows you to buy a decent home wherever you are stationed with 0% down payment with a VA Loan or 3.5% down payment with an FHA Loan.

Each tenant will live in their own unit, providing more privacy.

Main idea:
- Buy a two, three, or four-unit complex each year.
- Rent out the units you are not living in. The rent from the other tenants will replace most of your mortgage payment for the entire building (ideally, the combined rents are equal to or greater than your mortgage).

1stLt Jones decides to do a little more research prior to checking in to his squadron at MCAS New River. When he starts preparing to PCS, he realizes that his home does not have enough equity for a conventional loan refinance. Because of this, his best option at the new duty station is to use an FHA Loan to buy the next house. He has saved between $15,000 - $20,000 while at flight school, which is exactly what he needs for his FHA Loan down payment.

After calling several brokers, he made an offer on a four-unit complex near Sneads Ferry, NC and closed on the deal forty-five days later for $460,000.

The property already had three of the four units leased to tenants, so 1stLt Jones simply moved into the fourth unit. Here is how it worked out for him:

- Jones's mortgage was just under $2,650 every month.
- The tenants paid $900 a month for rent and a flat $50 utility fee. This added up to $2,850 a month and easily covered Jones' mortgage payment.
- He saved all his BAH and after twelve months had enough money to refinance the property and buy another multifamily complex with another VA Loan (or FHA Loan).
- 1stLt Jones handed his first four-unit property off to a good property manager.
- With all four units leased he makes approximately $600 in cash flow a month.
- He is also gaining about $500-$600 a month in equity for the first several years (this number is rising every month).

1stLt Jones goes through this process another three times by refinancing each loan into a conventional loan after they are seasoned for a year; thus, freeing up his FHA eligibility. By the time he leaves North Carolina, he is making around $2,000 of cash flow a month from 16 total units. His equity is growing at a steady $28,000 a year.

Vacation Rentals

Vacation rentals are a great way to house hack. Popular businesses in this space, like VRBO® and Airbnb®, have taken the vacation rental market by storm and have given hotels a run for their money. Because these models don't require companies to build tall buildings in desirable places, this modern house hack gives the homeowner (or investor) the ability to transform the empty space in their home into a money-making machine.

To succeed with this type of hack, all it really takes is some vision, structure and a little creativity to get things going well. If you are considering using vacation rentals to house hack, make sure you research your local rules, ordinances, laws and CC&R and HOA restrictions. You'll also want to talk with other investors who have been using this strategy in your local market. If you are uncertain about how to check other vacation rental listings and get ahold of another owner, or how to find an investor, go to a local real estate Meetup and ask around.

Once you are certain you want to use this potentially very lucrative house hacking method, proceed with the steps below.

STEP 1: Have a Vision

First, you must determine which features of your home-turned-investment may be attractive to prospective short-term tenants.

Consider the following questions:

- How many rooms do you intend to rent? The whole property or just a portion?
- Will you rent it only during the summer or winter (short-term)? Or can you rent it to tenants throughout the year (long-term, multiple tenants)?
- What type of tenants to you intend to attract? Business people? Vacation-goers?
- What features about the house (location, amenities, price) may attract that tenant or the desired duration of stay?
- How profitable can this become vs. the amount of work you will need to put in (turnover, cleaning costs, damage, etc.)?

These are just some the base-level questions you need to answer before you list your home on a vacation rental site. The strategy you put together sets the foundation for what you do next. If you decide to live in the home while you rent it, you'll be limited to renting out any extra space you have in the home. This could potentially be a loft, a spare bedroom, or even just a sofa. With Airbnb for instance, whatever extra space you have available to rent in your home will suffice. If you decide to rent your entire place, either while on deployment or if you have an extra unit on your property, you will have more options for *how* you rent and to whom you choose to rent.

The location of the property can make a difference in the crowd that it attracts. If your property is by the beach, you might expect to draw families or large groups. If your rental is in the heart of downtown in a major city, you might expect a younger crowd or tourists that want to explore the area. So, make sure you have thought this through before you begin to decorate, take pictures and actively advertise.

Knowing how often and time of year you want to rent the property to transient occupants is another critical point in mapping out your vision. If you are looking to rent the property seasonally, when you are on deployment, temporary duty for a military school, or all year, you will need to make sure your listing accurately reflects your intentions. You will need to know exactly what dates are available and that the price will be per night. We will cover more during the scheduling portion of this tutorial.

Action Steps:

1. Decide if you want to rent your entire home, a spare unit, or just a portion of your home.

2. Do research on local attractions near you. List five things people may want to see and do locally and include the activities in the listing.

3. Think about the types of tenants your property will attract. Identify three groups of people that may want to rent your property. List five things to incorporate into your rental that may entice each group.

STEP 2: Structure the Business

Once you have decided who your target market is and how you want to rent your property, it's time to start setting things up. The first things you need to put into place are a company or group of people to call to fix problems (this might be a property manager if you need one), maybe a handyman, and a system or protocol for how you want to operate. Having a Standard Operating Procedure (SOP) checklist will allow you to automate a lot of what you will be expected to do for each tenant and/or property.

If you are still active duty, one of the likely challenges you will run into with an active vacation rental is having limited to no communication when you are on duty, training, deployed or at sea. For this reason, an SOP and a trustworthy friend, partner or spouse could be of great benefit. He or she can run all the operations of the business while you are fulfilling your obligations to your job. Their responsibilities could include communicating with the tenants, scheduling bookings, handling the activity logs, calling service professionals to fix issues and making sure the property is clean during tenant turnover. Whoever this makeshift property manager is, it is important for them to be organized, responsible, and good at customer service. Even if you only expect to be gone a short period of time, consider having this person on standby just in case.

In this business, as you may find out, it only takes one bad review to have a very negative effect on your rental. So, make sure you cover your six and have the right people in place to handle the job. Whether that is a professional property manager or a responsible friend, be prepared.

If you consider yourself "handy" with repairs around the home, you can save yourself some serious money. You can expect, with a high volume of tenants rotating through your property, there are bound to be a few mishaps, damaged or lost items, plumbing issues and more. If you are not much of a do-it-yourselfer, you should start looking at service professionals in your area prior to advertising the rental. There may be local Airbnb management companies that offer a full range of services for your business. Consider these companies as they will be a one-stop-shop for everything you need. If you do find the need for professional management, just make sure you factor that into the daily/weekly/monthly rent to cover your bases.

Here are some must-have service providers if you choose to manage the property yourself:

- Plumber
- Electrician
- Handyman
- Cleaning Service

NOTE: You can always charge a cleaning fee to your tenants to recoup the costs of turnover - this is very common. In case of major repairs, you can withhold a portion of their security deposit for things that go beyond normal wear and tear.

Once you have your management and maintenance teams in place, you'll want to create a system. How are you going to operate your rental? What is the minimum amount of nights you will require guests to book? How many days in advance will you want them to book? How many days will they have to cancel without penalty? How many days will you leave in between tenant turnover? These are some of the questions you'll need to have answers to before you start operating. As you answer them, think about how tying in maintenance and cleaning will work.

What if your cleaning team is not available? Do you have a backup team? In addition, come up with a process for an emergency. How or who will you call? How will the situation be handled? Talking to other investors that have done vacation rentals in your community can be helpful and may give you insight you would not have otherwise considered.

Action Steps:

1. Talk to at least three people that do vacation rentals in your area. Get their advice on how to handle maintenance, management, and tenant turnover.

2. Decide whether you are going to manage the property yourself or hire some help.

3. Find good service professionals in the area and communicate with them on how you wish to run your business. You can to ask for discounts with continued use of their services. Find backup crews in case of emergency.

STEP 3: Be Creative

Now that you have your structure in place, it is time to get to the fun part. It is time to turn your vision into a reality. Use your creativity and find some good furnishings, decorations, and amenities to make your listing the best it can possibly be. Remember, you want to highlight the features and benefits that you wrote down in Step 1. If you struggle in the creativity department, it can be helpful to refer to HGTV or Pinterest.

When furnishing your home, you can save money by shopping at sites like OfferUp, Craigslist, or take a trip to Home Goods or a thrift store. You should *never* overpay for your furnishings due to the amount of wear and tear they are going to receive from your tenants. Your household items will wear at a faster rate, so keep that in mind as you shop.

Look for furnishings that will best match what you want your rental to look like. If you are into refurbishing old furniture (or maybe shabby-chic is your thing) the thrift shop or a flea market may be the perfect place for you to go shopping. Always see if you can haggle down prices to save a few more dollars and boost your return on investment. You would be surprised at how much you can save just by asking.

Don't hold back on filling your property up with important amenities. Refer back to your vision and think about what your target market will want to see. Do you have spices in your kitchen? Do you have extra linens? Do you offer soap, razors, or feminine products? What about good Wi-Fi? Today, having Wi-Fi is an absolute must, unless your listing is in the middle of nowhere and you are purposely advertising it as an opportunity to get off the grid.

It is beneficial to fill your property with important provisions that a non-vacation rental might have. If you live on a beach or lake, it may be a good idea to provide flotation devices or water sports toys. Do you have spices in the kitchen? Is there soap and toilet paper in the restrooms? What about Wi-Fi? You want your tenants to say, "they thought of everything!" There is a strong likelihood the tenant will forget something, so when they see you have it on hand you will have exceeded their expectations. This is how you get great reviews and repeat business.

Once you have your place looking like an HGTV model home, you're ready for a photographer to come and bring it to life. You would be amazed how professionals can make a place look by the proper placement of photos. If you have a good camera, make sure the photos are well lit and full of color. If your kitchen or bathroom are white, be sure to add a few items that are bright and vibrant to make the listing pop. Most people choose vacation rentals over hotels because they like the warm feeling of being home, so make sure your pictures capture that your vacation rental is warm and inviting. And make sure you turn on all the lights!

Action Steps:

1. Make a list of all the essential items you will need for your rental. Look at stores like Costco, Sam's

Club or Walmart to save on buying smaller items in bulk (toothpaste, shampoo, tissues, etc.)

2. Look online or at "economy" stores for discounted items or furniture other people are selling. Craigslist, Thrift Store and the like.

3. Hire a photographer to take quality photos of your place when you are done decorating.

NOTE: For safety, make sure to have safety items including a fire extinguisher, smoke detector, CO2 sensor, etc. in the property.

STEP 4: Listing the Vacation Rental

Advertising your property is the fourth and final step. This is surprisingly easier than you think. Be sure to follow the steps on the website of your choice to make the process a bit smoother. Sites like Airbnb.com or VRBO.com will pretty much run you through their process by the numbers. Three of the most important things you'll want to spend time on, to catch the eye of a potential tenant, are as follows: your cover photo, the amount you'll charge per night and the minimum number of nights your tenants can book.

Choosing a cover photo is a bigger deal than you might think. Keep in mind the cover photo is the first thing, along with price, your customers will see. You want something that will attract your target tenant to click on your listing. It is important to make sure that photo is either bright, vibrant, or has some curious or quirky features. Good pictures to use are landscapes, artwork, or maybe surrounding attractions in the area.

The next thing people will see, almost simultaneously with the photo, is your listing price. This is also important to get right. The best way to make sure you are not over-charging is to look at comparables in your area. Run a search to see what others are charging for a similar listing. You will want to consider the number of beds, whether it is a listing for a single room or for a whole house and maybe even what amenities are offered.

You should ensure the price accurately reflects what is expected in your area, but also understand that price can dictate the quality of tenants you receive. Keep this in mind if you list your price lower than the current market rate. Human nature tells us the less money people spend on things, the less value they will place on it, thus, the less they will take care of it. For these reasons, be sure not to undervalue your rental or the service you are providing.

One of the most critical steps in your listing is the process by which your tenants will complete their bookings. Convenience will drive momentum as your listing continues to gain traction and inquiries start to come in more frequently. You need to decide whether your guests can book automatically or if they need to contact you first. Most websites will require guests to have two forms of identification and to initiate a qualification process to confirm bookings automatically. Therefore, if you trust the system, allowing tenants to book your listing automatically will increase the speed of your bookings. Automatic verification is not a bad move if you are trying to maximize as many bookings as possible. If you are trying to regulate who comes into your property, stick to vetting all the potential tenants personally. This way, you will be able to get to know the tenants before they book the property.

Action Steps:

1. Choose the best cover photo you can to entice prospective tenants to view your listing over others.

2. Analyze the listings in your area that best compare to your home. Determine a competitive price range that will work for your listing.

3. Decide if you want people to book automatically or if you want to vet every tenant as they book.

At this point, you are ready to go! Make sure you track your renters and keep a cool head when things don't go 100% according to plan. If you manage your expectations and understand that you will spend your first experience learning more than profiting, you will be pleasantly surprised with how things turn out.

Other Value-add Hacks

So far, we have unearthed some valuable house hacking tools to use for your typical single-family and small multifamily units. Some of these are well-known to people with some real estate investing experience and some are unique to you, the veteran or active duty service member.

You will hear some more great testimony later in this book, but first, here are some value-add hacks that can be a game changer to the bottom line - which very few people think of when getting started.

First, consider a scenario in which a soldier used a VA Loan (again, zero down) to buy a four-plex near post. The two-story property is situated on a semi-busy street on one acre and the building is otherwise surrounded by grass. This type of property, size of lot, and location was specifically sought out by the service member. Other than the benefits we have already covered in this book, here are some other streams of income that can add to your monthly revenue.

- Dog park - if there is a small area that can be enclosed inexpensively with chain-link fencing, this amenity could encourage pet owners to rent from you.

- Pet rent - people will spend almost anything on their pets. You can charge a non-refundable pet deposit (for example, $350) and a monthly pet rent. Depending on your area, that could be an extra $15-$50/month.

- Cell tower leases - may be a stretch, but call your local cell service providers and ask if there is demand for leasing a portion of your land for a new cell tower.

- Covered parking - a paid luxury to protect against sun, snow, hail, etc.

- Ratio Utility Billing Service (RUBS) - this is starting to dive a little more into the "commercial" multifamily realm, but if you are paying water, sewer, electric and/or gas bills as an owner, you could use this system to bill-back the other three tenants. Your local market will dictate whether tenants will pay this or not so do some research to see if this is a viable option.

- Storage - you have plenty of land in this case, so either build a shed or go to Home Depot, buy an 8'x10' shed, section it off inside and rent out each area to tenants. If you have a basement, you can portion it off as well.

- Laundry machines - there are companies that will pay you a fee to lease machines to your tenants. Or if you are lucky enough to have a laundry room on a four-unit property, that is cash in the bank!

- Vending machines - if there is a safe, sheltered breezeway and an outlet you could make some extra money. There are even gumball/non-perishable candy machine companies (no power required) that will split profits.

- Trash valet - this sounds ridiculous, but if you have a tenant who needs this service, you can offer to pick up their garbage from outside their door for a reasonable fee.

- Play structure/BBQ - another amenity to attract tenants and charge (potentially) higher rent. *NOTE: Get insurance!*

- Simple "Tech Package" - small convenience, but for $25 you can install a USB outlet in the kitchen and/or other outlets. Tenants may even want touch-key door locks if it is offered. You charge $5-$10/month for this.

- Renter's insurance - there are companies that will offer a "revenue share" if you get your tenants to use their insurance.

- Billboards - I have a good friend who said he has a rental with some land on a back-road highway on the way to a nearby military installation. He said he needed to increase the property income or sell. I suggested he build a couple small makeshift billboards and spray paint "Your Ad Here" with his phone number. $50/month per sign can add up and it also helps the advertiser!

- Solar Hacking - the premise is simple: generate excess solar power and sell it back to your electric company. You will likely want to purchase a property that already has solar installed (not leased). These systems are not cheap, so the numbers would have to work for you both short and long-term.

There are limitless amenities, upgrades, or services an owner can offer to increase the net operating income. This small list shows the multitude of value-add strategies you can employ if you are creative with all your property has to offer.

House Hacking: Real-Life Examples

Tim's Story

After purchasing my first primary residence back in 2011, I became more and more interested in real estate investing. I knew there were many ways someone could make money with real estate, but I had no idea where to begin.

It all started by thinking it was pretty cool that I could personally renovate my own house with some basic upgrades and then be rewarded by its value increasing. Real estate investors call this adding "sweat equity" or more formally, "forced appreciation."

My growing interest in real estate investing and personal finance led me to become a Navy Command Financial Specialist (CFS). I loved being a CFS because of the continual opportunity to learn more about money and wealth and help other service members improve their financial situation.

My first "ah-ha" moment came once I discovered the world of podcasts. BiggerPockets and a few other great shows added immeasurable value to my personal journey.

As many real estate investors will admit, a wonderful little purple book is what really pushed them into taking a massive leap towards real estate investing. I stumbled across *Rich Dad Poor Dad* and it essentially consumed me. My interest in real estate and building wealth exploded! I never looked back.

House Hack #1 - Accidental House Hack

I used my VA Loan to close on my first primary home in 2011. The home was in a great neighborhood and was in a growing part of town with constant development and gentrification. The house was unique because it had two master bedrooms. One was on the second level, where my wife and I slept, and one was on the lower level where we anticipated our family would stay when they came to visit.

The extra space in the home, coupled with my passion for real estate and finance, sparked the idea of simply renting out the lower level to a trusted individual who was looking for a rental in that area. We found a great roommate and the timing could not have been better. I was deployed early that year, so my wife enjoyed having company around, plus they helped pay more than half the mortgage payment!

It is funny looking back today because we house hacked without even realizing it. I simply thought I bought a house that was too big, but it turned out to be a great introduction to house hacking. In fact, I was experiencing the power of real estate investing firsthand.

After our first roommate had moved on, we had no problems finding someone to move in immediately, mostly due to the nice area and perfect size of the room we were renting. So, there we were, hooked!

House Hack #2 - Fourplex Using a 203k Loan!

Soon after our first house hack, and after diving head first into real estate investment education, books, and more podcasts, I learned about the 203k Loan. This is an FHA-backed loan that allows you to "wrap" (include) rehab costs into the price of the home, only requires a 3.5% down payment, and can be used on any property from one to four units. The only catch is that you must occupy one of the units.

This is considered an owner-occupied loan (like the VA Loan), whereas the borrower must have the "intent" to move into the house or one of the units for at least six months and one day.

We were able to find a fourplex to execute this new strategy and I must tell you – we were excited!

Here are the rough numbers:

- Purchase price = $145,000
- Rehab budget = $100,000
- Down Payment = $15,000

- Total loan amount = $230,000

Originally, the rehab was scheduled to take no more than ninety days. I was surprised that the bank and the general contractors agreed to the renovation plan and timeline, especially with $100,000 of work to be done! But they agreed, we closed on time, and I was scheduled to move in shortly after.

Since the rehab would take some time, and I had recently PCS'd from another state, I had to find a short-term rental in the area. Yes, I had to pay rent where I was living, as well as the mortgage on the fourplex. Yes, I needed to have liquid capital to make this possible. But getting four completely renovated units for $15,000 was well worth the effort!

In the end, because of some permitting issues and construction delays, the rehab ended up taking eight months and I never actually got to move into this new fourplex hack. But, eventually, my wife and I realized that we were happy where we lived during those eight months of renovations, so we decided to stay put and to rent out the last of the four units which we had initially intended on moving into.

It is now a very nice cash-flowing fourplex and I look to refinance it into a commercial investment loan very soon.

House Hack #3 - Triplex with a VA Rehab Loan

Believe it or not, there are banks out there that offer a VA Rehab Loan. This means your 0% down payment will cover both a house and all the renovation costs! What?!

This is an amazing benefit to those who have served and if you are even considering getting involved in the real estate game, this opportunity really begs the question: "why not?"

Even with a family, there are plenty of small multifamily properties that are nice, two- or three-bedroom units that will be very compatible with family living. Even better, you may find separate, detached dwellings so you will not have to share walls, which seems to be one of the biggest turn-offs for individuals thinking about doing this.

In this situation I was able to find a perfect single-family home for my family, in one of the most desirable neighborhoods, best school district, *AND* with a completely detached duplex in the back! Moreover, it sits on a large corner lot, so the house and the duplex are facing different streets. No one would ever know the owner of the home also owns the duplex! It's a great set-up.

Again, this was a 0% down payment VA Loan and I was able to wrap in $70,000 of renovation costs as part of the deal. I did, however, have to bring about $6,000 to close, but again, well worth it!

As it stands now, I'm really looking forward to when the rehab on all three units is complete, so I can rent out each duplex unit for $850-$950 and basically live for free! That's really house hacking at its best. It's a great feeling knowing that the home I'm living in is not a major financial liability like it is for many other people I know.

The beautiful thing about hacking your housing, it puts you at an incredible advantage to take your real estate business to the next level. Not only will you become a homeowner, an investor, and a landlord, but you'll also be able to get paid to live and literally stack up capital at an accelerated pace! This, in turn, will quickly put you in the position to grow your buy-and-hold rental portfolio.

Key takeaways:

- When you house hack, you can become a homeowner, investor, landlord, and a property manager all in one deal!
- Like a VA Loan, you must intend to occupy the property when using a 203K Loan. This can get you in trouble if you do not.

- You must have a solid financial foundation established before you can begin this journey. I cannot stress this enough.

- You must have a support system and a team of people who have your back. As it turns out, Active Duty Passive Income can provide the financial education AND support you need to be successful!

Eric's Story

I will preface my story by saying, my life's purpose and my passion is not to be rich. On the contrary, it is to educate, empower and to help people grow. This is what drives me. It's the reason I chose to become an enlisted soldier after attending college. What I have discovered through the Active Duty Passive Income community is that I get to combine two of my passions, real estate and mentorship, to fulfill that mission.

"Ah ha!", I shouted in my head. I had the most enlightening and powerful thought of my life – I was going to get rich . . . slowly.

In fact, I've had two similar moments that affected me so profoundly that I was sure I would succeed. Ok, so maybe one of them was the result of too much coffee one morning, but that doesn't change the impact of that moment for me.

I hope, in reading this book and getting involved with the Active Duty Passive Income community, you too will find your epiphany – whatever it takes to get started. Because if I did it - you can too.

Epiphany Moment #1:

There I was in late 2014, listening to the audio version of *Rich Dad, Poor Dad* in my truck just prior to attending one of those "guru" single-family house flipping seminars you always hear about. In preparation for the event, I was listening to the book, so I thought, hoping to hit the ground running in a ballroom full of professional investors. I had heard from someone that it was a good read, so I thought, "What the heck, why not?" Side note: I have to say, now I love *Rich Dad, Poor Dad* and recommend it for anyone. Period. It doesn't matter if real estate is your thing or not. I found myself immersed in the story and halfway through the book I wanted to *be* Rich Dad. I thought, "He makes it sound so simple. I can do that!" Now, off to my first real estate training event that I was certain would launch my future success.

Epiphany Moment #2:

This was the too-much-coffee moment. Nevertheless, it represented an important mindset shift.

After the house flipping seminar, I had moved on from merely dreaming about flipping houses in the San Francisco Bay Area to reading a string of "mindset" books (to get my mind into an entrepreneurial focus). I wanted to start taking action but knew I needed a solid foundation first. I read *Think and Grow Rich* by Napoleon Hill and *The Millionaire Mind* by Thomas J. Stanley. About three quarters through Millionaire Mind, I had this moment that just kind of hit me like a ton of bricks: I will be a millionaire! I then found myself loudly repeating, as prompted by the author, "I have a millionaire mind! I have a millionaire mind!" That may sound cheesy and it certainly felt as much, but at that moment, there were *no* limitations on my mind.

More importantly, this is where I decided I no longer care what anyone else says or thinks about my future – it's not their future, it's mine! I will succeed in real estate. It was decided.

My Personal Version of the Military House Hack

If you are an Active Duty Soldier, Sailor, Airman, Marine, Coast-Guardian, Space Cadet or veteran, you have one big advantage over everyone else in the world. What is it? You may not have money to invest in real estate yet, but you have one absolutely *amazing* capital-building tool through the power of the VA Loan.

When I was stationed at Hunter Army Airfield in Savannah, GA, we purchased a new construction single-family home for around $150,000. My wife and I got it under contract while I was on my first rotation to Iraq in 2006. Initially, we were nervous about out-of-pocket expenses, but ultimately we were able to use my first VA Loan eligibility, put zero down and even roll the VA funding fee (2%) and closing costs into the loan.

That property ended up becoming a rental from 2010 until 2018 when I sold it for a profit. I'll also mention that since I put zero dollars into it, every dollar I made each month from it over the eight years was technically an infinite return. The idea that you can own an asset producing cash each month, year after year, and have NO MONEY in the deal was very exciting.

In early 2011, I left a career in 160th Special Operations Aviation Regiment and headed back to the San Francisco Bay Area for a job that paid just enough to get by but was near my wife's family. It was a great company and a good opportunity for me to transition smoothly from the Army to civilian life, but I had no idea how expensive the Bay Area was going to be!

Fast forward two years: we had been renting a house and saving money when my wife got pregnant with our second son. Since we had taken the time in the years leading up to now following the Dave Ramsey-mentality and getting completely out of debt, we were now ready to enter the REALLY expensive Bay Area real estate market. Well, we thought we were ready. But we were thankful to have a solid financial foundation, which made all the difference.

After attending the previously discussed flipping bootcamp (and subsequent advanced course "upsell"), I was led to deciding on how to proceed. But one thing I consistently recognized as most important - taking action! Since I was not yet poised to "flip" in the Bay Area, I had to think up a way to start investing given my specific circumstances.

Here are the three strategies, in chronological order, that began our five-year journey "hacking" our way to success with the VA Loan. Pay attention from here!

Before you continue, let me preface the explanation of my experiences by stating what you will inevitably be thinking, "Well, 2012 was a good time to buy real estate." It sure was. But for those of you who read this and say, "well you caught the market at the right time," we may be headed towards similar times and by reading below and getting educated now, you are taking the next steps towards being ready yourself!

My recommendation is to act now. Get educated and execute your strategy when the time is good for you. As I write this in 2018, I know there will be market downturns to come. I'm expecting it, I'm ready for it, and I'm excited about it! You should be too. Especially if you are or were a member of the Armed Forces.

First Hack: VA Loan, All Market Appreciation (2+ years ownership):

In late 2012 we bought the first home. Notice I called it a "home", not a "house" or "property," as one would normally say for an investment. We had originally intended to stay in this home. It was a beautiful, newer, four-bedroom, three-bathroom "duet" (which is an attached two-story property, kind of like a townhouse-duplex). It also happened to be a short sale, where the owner had been relocated to Texas for work and the previous buyer had fallen through. The house was listed at a price we thought we could barely afford, almost the cheapest home on the market at the time, but we also knew the market was appreciating and it was in a great neighborhood with good schools.

For a kid from Iowa, who'd only used a VA Loan to buy that relatively inexpensive house in Georgia so far, I had major, major sticker shock! Do construction materials cost five times more in California? I digress. The cool part about this property is that it was in great shape, had all the original builder upgrades, and needed no work at all. So, we got pre-approved for a VA Loan and offered full asking price the same day we saw it. Now here's where it gets good. Since there were almost no comps for a duet built in 2008, we ended up getting the home for what it appraised for, which was $50K *less* than our offer!

In 2014, after owning this property for two years – and after just starting to learn about how to invest in real estate, we contacted an agent to see what it was now worth. To our surprise, it had appreciated 36%! And since we owned the property more than two years, if we sold it, we would pay NO tax on any net gains. You can do the math, but that was one heck of a great investment. The point is not to call this strategy a "hack", but more to note that without the VA Loan, I never would have been able to enter the Bay Area real estate market. What an amazing benefit!

We now had a good bit of money for a down payment on our next "home," but my point-of-view on real estate had changed forever.

Second Hack: Conventional Loan, All Forced Appreciation (less than 1-year ownership):

As we were in the process of selling the first house, we were taking our kids tide-pooling in the Northern Monterey Bay area one day when we stumbled across an open house in a nearby little beach town. This house was two blocks from a local beach, so the location was great. It was a four-bedroom, two-bathroom property that was outdated, but it had no major issues and we could see that with some TLC it would be a beautiful spot to live. Since my salary had risen at my job, I felt comfortable stretching our finances a bit while using the new-found profits from the last house for the down payment. After all, I was once again *certain* this was our forever dream home.

We put in an offer for the full asking price and it was accepted! Surprised, my wife and I quickly dreamed up plans to make necessary upgrades using some of the profits from the first house, but then two things occurred. First, we realized this house had a weird layout. Second, we had a few conversations with neighbors and found that the neighborhood was slowly starting to turn over into an area of out-of-town retirees who wanted their *retirement* dream home.

"Ah ha! An exit strategy!" I immediately thought (but kept to myself). We could make sure we had this buyer-type in mind as we started renovations! I can't say this was a thought my wife had, but I couldn't help myself. I was thinking strategically about real estate now.

This in mind, we started by removing an odd centrally-located bedroom (thus, converting the house into a 3/2) which then opened space that extended the master bathroom by six feet and added four feet of new space in the main living area near the kitchen. Remove a bedroom? Why would anyone ever do that? Seems like it would devalue the property, right? Not for a retiree who wants to live by the beach and only needs three bedrooms!

After about six weeks, roughly $50,000, some sweat, and a lot of trips to Home Depot, the renovation was complete. We now had a beautiful, large master bathroom and an open floor concept. The kitchen was completely updated with cabinets and quartz counters. The interior was painted with Spanish Sand and Sea Breeze Blue colors to give it a great beach vibe. Outside, I stained the concrete driveway myself, epoxied the garage floor and installed a cool copper outdoor shower with beautiful tile work that made rinsing off after a day at the beach a breeze.

I'll insert a cool fact here: remember that flipping seminar I went to? Well, one of the contractors that I met at the event became a good friend and agreed to only charge labor and materials on the renovation! When I applied for permits for the work, the city valued the rehab at $180,000. This goes to show how important networking is. You never know who you will meet!

The valuation on the renovation also made me curious to see what the property was now worth, so I contacted the listing agent from whom we had bought the property from to see what he thought. Fast forward two weeks; we got a full price, all cash offer from – you guessed it – a retiree from San Diego. There's more to the story, but it felt like a blink of an eye.

In only nine months' time the property had appreciated 29% and sold at a higher price point than the first house. Having owned this house less than one year, we were able to capitalize on forced appreciation (the rehab) alone, but the exit was a little more complicated.

Typically, one would have to pay short-term capital gains tax of close to 34% on net profit, but because my employer thought it was best that I move about seventy miles away, I ended up not owing any tax. Had I needed to, I would have paid the tax and it still would have been an amazing profit.

NOTE: You should always consult a CPA when complicated scenarios arise.

Third Hack: Combination of Forced and Market Appreciation (exactly 366-day ownership)

Third time's the charm? We sure hoped so! To be honest, every time we moved into any of these homes, we wanted them to be "the one" that we would stay in forever. Since I'm handy and always thinking about real estate, they all ended up as live-in flips. I couldn't help it and my wife is a *saint*! I owe all our success to her. These strategies take a patient, supportive spouse who can see the big picture, is willing to be agile, and who embraces adaptation, even with two kids. This shows that you can do it with kids too!

The final house we used the live-in-flip hack on was a four-bedroom, two-bathroom house with a pool, backed up to a 40-mile long bike trail and situated a block away from high-ranked and very desirable elementary school. We ended up putting $30,000 (again, money that came from both the original VA Loan hack as well as the beach house hack) into superficial upgrades including three new garage doors, all new pool equipment, stained concrete, crown molding, and more. Lots of sweat equity went into this one, and I did almost all the work myself.

I started thinking, why don't I look into selling this one *myself,* so I can save the commission? It's important to constantly think of how you can improve your position. How can you get creative to maximize profit? Solution: for $384, a couple dozen hours of studying and one state exam, I got my California Real Estate Salesperson license. Did I know what I was doing? Absolutely not. But I wanted to be bold, courageous, and continue to learn. Plus, the incentive to save the commission on a million-dollar home in the Bay Area was enough to get me over my nerves.

After simply posting the house on Zillow's "Make Me Move" and adding two open house times in one weekend, I found an interested buyer who was not yet represented by an agent! He offered full price, my broker worked up the paperwork (I only had to pay one-half percent) and I ended up saving $70,000 on commissions.

This third house, which had already appreciated by 10%, was sold in 366 days. Coincidence? Nope. I knew that at the 366-day mark I would only have to pay *long*-term capital gains (as opposed to short-term). So, by delaying the closing (contractually) until that day, I saved about another 15% on what otherwise would have been close to 34% tax. Once we closed, I had my CPA calculate what taxes I owed Uncle Sam and I cut a check immediately.

If you are going to try this strategy you can mitigate some risk by keeping in mind that all these houses had one thing in common: a great LOCATION and at least some desirable feature(s). This always helps with appreciation and attractiveness to sellers and will make your journey a little easier if you keep that in mind.

This part of my investment career is what I refer to as my "capital-building phase." Since then, I have expanded my real estate portfolio to include Self-Directed IRA investments, tax liens, private lending, out-of-state turnkey rentals, a large mobile home park syndication and some small multifamily units. After learning about and investing in all these strategies, I plan to focus on large multifamily deals moving forward.

I'll leave you with this; if you are curious about how to get started in the real estate investing business, I'll recommend a couple first steps. First, find a community with a similar mindset that is full of people who want to help you, in your particular situation. Anyone who has been in the real estate industry long enough should tell you the same thing: it's a team sport. At least that's what I believe. The next piece of advice I'll give is what I would tell myself if I could go back in time ten or fifteen years: house hack your primary residence. Your future self will thank you.

Mike's Story

When it came to financial literacy, like most Americans, I was illiterate. I never had a role model I looked up to financially. I grew up in a poor family in a very low-income community. I had a lot of love, but money was never something we spoke about because it was always a hard conversation. I grew up thinking it was rude and awkward to talk with people about their finances and I was expected to never ask. I liked the idea of having a financially knowledgeable figure in my life, but financial mentorship was not something I thought was possible.

The first four years of my Naval career were spent in Sasebo, Japan without much of a thought towards my future. When I wasn't busy learning how to be a Division Officer on one of the smallest and "baddest" warships in the fleet, I was mostly partying and adventuring in the "Land of the Rising Sun." But when the time came to PCS, I couldn't stop thinking, "what do I do next?" and, "what did I accomplish in the last four years?"

I am a very driven guy, so this first tour left me with a pretty sour taste for the Navy - not because the Navy had let me down, but because I had not really focused on personal development at all.

Because I was struggling with finding any harmonious intersection between personal growth and being a Naval Officer, I really started spending some time thinking about what I would do when I ETS (Expiration of Time in Service). At that same time, even though I knew my likelihood of staying in twenty years was slim, I didn't want any limitations on my second tour before it even started. For that reason alone, I committed to making a change.

I evaluated my personal skills, beliefs, wants and desires and reflected on where I was financially at the time. After a thorough self-analysis, I discovered I had already accrued a bunch of unnecessary debt, I had zero cash-producing assets and nothing positive to carry forward into my next quarter of life. Yes, I had a good paying job and while I was grateful for that, it was a difficult realization (once I had recognized I had nothing) to feel like a slave to my organization. I'm sure some of you can relate. I just felt like I was going nowhere. Or like the term Robert Kiyosaki famously coined, I was "in the rat race" of life.

My epiphany moment came in 2016. I turned to God. I asked him to renew my spirit and show me a way to achieve the happiness I was searching for. Regardless of your religion or beliefs, I think it is important to hold a perspective that places someone or something in higher regard than yourself. Believe in something great.

I prayed for Him to educate me, to put me on the path I needed to take in life and to open my eyes to opportunities I didn't see before. Since I didn't really feel like the military was my calling, I felt I needed some external enlightenment. Slowly but surely, He did just that. If you are struggling as I did, I hope you can find the same clarity and direction. It changed my life.

The first discovery that led me to where I am today: podcasts! I knew that podcasts were "a thing" while I was in Japan because I used to listen to a DJ on a radio station that talked about them all the time. However, I didn't know they were also for information-gathering. It completely blew my mind when I found people were sharing new ideas, data, and stories from all over the world, from walks of life, spreading all kinds of information. With this new-found love of learning through podcasts, I was ready to soak up all the info I could! I was hooked. As I write this, I should add that I'm now hosting my own podcast: "Military Real Estate Investing."

The next God-given gift that pushed me along in my journey was learning to network. He introduced people into my life that would become a catalyst for my personal growth. I started getting into the business and investment mindset through a friend who introduced me to a Multi-Level Marketing (MLM) company. She then connected me with someone who, even though I have since given up the MLM strategy, is still a mentor to me today. This mentor then introduced me to educational audiobooks and motivational speakers. Since I hated to read, you can see where this is going. One thing led to the next. With this new source of knowledge, I started becoming aware of who I was, what I wanted and what action steps I was or could be taking. Success followed.

Up to this point in life, the concept of sitting down to read a book had never appealed to me. A news article or magazine, maybe, but something about sitting in one place reading a book always put me to sleep. With podcasts and audiobooks, I could now "read" while I was working out, driving, or working on the ship. Motivational speakers were awesome because they were the perfect boost I needed for improving my mood on a bad day.

Networking and getting to know and work with other like-minded people, may be the most important part of real estate investing. So far it had gotten me focused, inspired and opened me up to a world of education and opportunity.

Somewhere along the line, my mentor mentioned a book called *Rich Dad, Poor Dad*, by Robert Kiyosaki. Because I was just getting started with audiobooks, I put it aside and marked it as "just another book to read when I get around to it." This book would eventually change the course of my life.

Months later, while on a team call, I heard one of my Commanders say something to the effect of, "don't let your past define who you are, use the models that are out there, then make your own story." The same gentleman also mentioned *Rich Dad, Poor Dad* as a great book to help shift and open your mindset. His impromptu speech got me thinking about my life, aspirations, ambitions, and which direction I was headed. And it was now the second time I'd heard a recommendation to read this book.

I finally read it. And if you haven't, add it to your queue immediately after finishing this book. The lessons I learned from *Rich Dad, Poor Dad*, like thousands of other investors and entrepreneurs, opened my eyes to the power of real estate and changed my life forever.

Fast forward six months from that date and I purchased my first real estate investment. After reading audiobooks and listening to podcasts, I knew I needed to act if I wanted to experience the most growth and learning in the real estate industry. I also knew that having a place to live, *and* a place to rent out was the way to start.

After some searching, I found a double condo on the beach in Norfolk, VA that I felt I could get started with. Using a creative strategy that I had learned through the podcasts and books I'd read, I negotiated with the seller and bought the top half of the building with a lease-option to buy the bottom half. The seller helped me find someone to lease the bottom and later, when my wife PCS'd to Virginia, we bought the bottom as well!

The Summer of our first year as investors we put the upper condo on Airbnb, which did very well. We made enough money to pay our mortgage for the full year! We then used the surplus of income, in combination with our wedding gift money to buy two additional investment properties.

One year later, only our second year of investing in real estate, we had almost doubled our profits. We then reinvested profits to buy a few more in the U.S., as well as our first foreign real estate investment while I was deployed. You can see, from my experience, how a little education, understanding, networking, and creativity can really snowball into something great.

As I type this, I just negotiated a seller-financed deal on an eight-unit next door that I plan to Airbnb. All of this is happening because I was willing to be comfortable being uncomfortable.

Final Thoughts:

We live in an age where information is not as limited as it was in the past. You truly can change the course of your life if you have the hunger and the desire to find out what is out there. You can produce massive results if you have the determination to put in the work and are willing to sacrifice superficial desires to accomplish your dreams.

You can find the answers you need - or at least your own epiphany moment - in our Military Real Estate Investing Academy, in our #StartTheSpark social media platform and community, or in books and podcasts just like we did. But it is time to stop watching other people live their best lives. Learn from them, get involved and live your best life too.

Remember that knowledge is power, but action is authority. Life is not like a narrow channel. There is no easy path and there will always be obstacles to overcome, which is why it is important to surround yourself with like-minded people. We are all in this together. That is why we do what we do for the ADPI Community.

Most importantly, along this journey I have met some awesome people and shared great experiences so far. Real estate investing has brought immense happiness to my life and I am excited for the opportunity to bring happiness to other people. That's YOU!

"On the strength of one link in the cable, depend on the might of the chain. Who knows when you'll be tested. So live that you'll bear the strain." - Fifth Law of the Navy

Adam's Story

My beautiful wife, Raquel, introduced me to the world of real estate investing through her family. My in-laws owned their home free and clear and they also owned a rental property. It was paid off and producing significant income. This planted a seed and opened my eyes to the real estate world.

Eventually, I dove into real estate education by absorbing every piece of literature, audiobook, or podcast I could find. As mentioned for others in this book, *Rich Dad, Poor Dad* was an amazingly motivating and inspirational book for me. I learned what an asset and a liability were, I learned where I wanted to focus my energy, and I learned my in-laws were making some sense! It took some time, but I discovered my own financial freedom number and began to understand what it would take to not have to rely on a military retirement. That number meant a lot to me because I was injured and unsure of where my military career would take me. I did not know if I would get medically boarded, medically retired or incur further injuries. I needed to get my family to a point where it did not matter what happened. I was determined to truly understand what my "why" was because that's what drives you through the challenges in life. Focusing on *why* you want to do this will make all the difference in the world. My family is my why.

After a lot of research, I determined that my strategy was not going to be buying single-family rental houses. While that works well for a lot of people and it is a very viable option, I was ambitious and wanted to speed up the process to reach my financial freedom number. I skipped right over single-family and small multifamily investing and went straight into apartment investing. My wife and I knew that we needed to set ourselves up for success and be smart with our money. So, we saved as much money as we could to be prepared to make the right decisions when the opportunity arose.

A strong point must be made before I continue: I started buying properties while stationed overseas! If I can manage to invest in apartments while on active duty and traveling all around the world, anyone can.

"Raquel, I am going to fly out to Los Angeles to go to a conference and meet some people," I proclaimed. I was overseas at the time, so this was not just a quick, cheap flight. I was committed to taking steps towards my goals and I wanted results badly. Thankfully, I have a very supportive wife who knew I had the best interest of my family in mind.

The best part of the trip was the amazing people I met. It was so cool to meet so many like-minded real estate enthusiasts. Many were less educated than me, but because they were just as motivated, we were rubbing elbows with experienced investors and making deals happen. I met some great people, but also found myself helping and teaching almost everyone I encountered. This gave me confidence. I realized I really absorbed a lot of what I researched but I knew I had not yet put it to use. It was time to jump in and take further steps towards my goals. It was time to take massive action!

I left Los Angeles more motivated than ever. I sent letters, hired virtual assistants, called more brokers, created partnerships, and continued my education. I entered a multifamily education program, I became an active participant in a mastermind group, and I got a highly experienced mentor. It is not an exaggeration when I say I analyzed probably more than 1,000 deals. Why did all this matter? These relationships are what sparked the first couple investments I made. The networking was more important that almost all the education I received before and I knew that fostering these relationships was going to pay off.

After several anxious months, I closed on my first deal, a 62-unit apartment! The relationships I built in L.A. and through my mastermind group, are what put together the partnership for this deal. We purchased the property for $1.2 million and planned to put in about $700,000 towards renovations. Based on our plans, the property will appraise for $2.6 million, on the low-end, after we complete repositioning.[3] I

---

[3] The process of changing a property cosmetically and financially. Many times, it

knew it would be a lot of work, but everything I had done to prepare was now coming into play. I was meeting people, running numbers, talking with lawyers and banks, working out schedules, and flying around the world to get it done. I was prepared, I was taking action, and my confidence was high.

After we closed the 62-unit deal I was more excited than ever. I wanted to find my next deal as soon as possible and after meeting some more investors, I decided to get into a syndication (a process by which a person puts a property under contract and finds investors to put money into the deal to complete the purchase). I found this deal through my mentor and they were treating it as an education platform as well. Through this syndication, I would be receiving a preferred rate of return on my investment, education on how a syndication works, more experience in apartment investing, and the ability to say I am an equity investor in another hundred and thirty-two units. I knew this investment was going to provide the ability learn the process and would present more syndication opportunities soon!

The excitement of taking on a new project is exhilarating. It drives me. And the understanding of the financial freedom this will bring someday down the road is unparalleled. I now know I will have the time

---

requires renovations, changing property managers, getting new tenants and raising rents.

and ability to take my kids on vacations, take a break from work during the summers, buy the plane I've always wanted, and no longer rely on my government paycheck.

My goals are written down and I am working toward achieving them every day. Reading books like this, staying engaged in communities like ADPI, and stepping out of my comfort zone has brought me closer to my goals than I ever could have done on my own.

Mitch's Story

Every time someone mentions real estate investing, I get this rush of energy that captures me and takes me back to when I was twenty years old sitting in Al Ramadi, Iraq, dreaming of the day that I would be able to purchase real estate. That was in 2005. My interest in real estate started when my father sent me local real estate listing magazines just for light reading material. Unbeknownst to him, he was creating droplets that would become my vast ocean in the real estate industry. While other people in my unit were reading Maxim Magazine, I was ripping out pages of the homes I liked and made lists of renovations that would raise their values. I was creating a dream board about real estate before I knew anything about dreamboarding.

After I returned home from my first deployment, I saved up $28,000. That was a great start, but I needed to dig deeper, I thought, if I was to become a successful real estate investor. At the same time, knowing I had to think creatively about how to make more or save more money, I discovered the incredible opportunity that allowed me to add an additional stream of income while still in the military.

That opportunity was BAH (Basic Allowance for Housing). I now had the choice to live on post and not receive BAH or live off post and collect BAH monthly.

I also realized if I found a roommate that was also collecting BAH and we rented a place together, it would mean that we would each have extra money to spend at the bar on the weekend. Win-win! So, I started cohabitation, not even knowing I was "house hacking." I just knew the numbers worked well. In fact, they worked so well that it wasn't long before we started renting the couch out just to earn a few extra bucks. Now the three of us were technically being *paid* to live off base *and* had more freedom than we would if we were living on post.

At the time, I was stationed at Fort Carson, Colorado but I had no plans to stay in the service after my contract finished. If I had, I would have used my VA Loan to buy a property and rent to my roommates. I seized part of the opportunity in front of me but did not take full advantage of the strategy simply because I didn't understand all my benefits and how to use them!

Six months later, I left active duty and re-enlisted into the Army Reserves, where I moved to Johnstown, PA. Shortly after that, I got married and bought a house using my VA Loan with my wife. Shortly after we married, my wife joined the Air Force and we had to relocate to Sumter, South Carolina. We were just seven months into our new mortgage, so our only option was to rent the property while we were away.

In South Carolina, I immediately started to network and ended up making friends with some like-minded folks in the Air Force. These guys were also house hacking similarly to the strategy I used at Ft. Carson. They were collecting BAH and renting out rooms in the same house. After a while, we realized it wasn't us who were the smart ones, the landlord was the real genius! It turns out, he was also in the military. We were paying down the mortgage principal every month and cash flowing the property for *him*, so he could hack *his* BAH. I remember the feeling in my stomach when it all clicked. I had a similar feeling to drinking a big milkshake and then going on a roller coaster! It was a good feeling but nauseating at the same time because I realized that *he* was benefiting the most.

What if I could buy a house with a VA Loan, 100% financing, use my BAH to cover my housing payment *and* rent out a room? Eventually, I did move back into my old house in Johnstown where I was able to rent out a room until I got deployed to Afghanistan. I was paying most of my mortgage payment by renting out a single room but was not receiving housing allowance (BAH) at the time. Imagine the extra income I would have made if I were still collecting BAH!

In 2012, I sat with my friend after a shift in Afghanistan, and my friend suggested that I do some reading. He handed me a book called *Think and Grow*

Rich by Napoleon Hill. This book had a huge impact on my life. What struck a chord in me from this book was the supposition that I needed a means to generate passive income or I would be working forever. Given my experience with rental house hacking and the increasing cash flow real estate provided me, I began my search for a second property. I knew people were renting properties in Colorado Springs because of the military base there, so I began searching for a "cash flowing property." As explained earlier in this book, in simple terms, the rental income generated would cover my expenses and give me a little extra cash each month.

If I could find one to buy, I planned to live in the house and have my tenants pay the bills for me. So, a couple weeks later, in the back of an MRAP in Afghanistan, I put a Purchase and Sales Agreement together on a fourplex. This was the 0% down opportunity that I had been waiting for. So, I timed my leave to go home and do a final walkthrough of the property just before closing.

The fourplex started off generating $1,000 per month cash flow. I was in business. Recently, we raised the rents again and the property now produces $1,600 per month. Depending on where you are on your real estate journey, this may seem like a lot or a little. For me, an extra $1,000 dollars per month gave me some breathing room and meant that I did not have to be overseas anymore if I did not want to. To this day I have no idea why I waited so long to get my second property. It took me four years to go from one property to five units.

After I acquired my second property, things got interesting. My eyes were focused on real estate and the potential it had to create income every single month. I left Afghanistan and decided I would buy a third property. However, when I applied for a loan, the banks told me that because I changed careers, I would not qualify to buy a property for two years, stating that they needed two years of paystubs. I refused to be disheartened and decided that if I would have to wait to buy properties, then I better get prepared for when they finally allow me to buy properties again.

So, in that two-year period, I started four companies, became a licensed Real Estate Agent and started an S-Corp for my investment properties. It was then that I also set a goal of purchasing a million dollars' worth of real estate in the next twelve months. I knew that if I owned a million dollars' worth of real estate, it would generate around $100,000 dollars a year. I had no idea how I was going to do it, but I put the goal on my phone, wrote it on my mirror, went on Facebook Live and told my friends and family what I was going to accomplish. From there, I bought, renovated, flipped and refinanced my way towards achieving my goal. I ended up buying $1.2 million worth of property in twelve months and that momentum put me on track to owning $2.3 million worth of property just four months later.

I would like to give you a million-dollar secret here. The way I was able to double my real estate holdings in four months was through teamwork. Remember earlier in this book we talked about the power and importance of networking? In order to generate massive amounts of wealth in real estate, or to speed up the process, you must build what I call "The Million-Dollar Team." I started off buying the properties on my own, which is why it took me so long to get my second property. Now, I have investment partners and formed a team of contractors, lenders, attorneys, property managers, and other key players. With this team, I was able to streamline the investment process. Real estate investing is a team sport, and you can go so far alone, but you can go so much farther and faster together.

As of 2018, I purchase a new property every three to six months and own over four hundred rental units. The rental properties I own allow me to travel up to six months of the year and I take month-long vacations to the Caribbean, which was always a dream of mine. The beautiful thing about real estate investing is you can do it from practically anywhere you have an internet connection. Because I have teams that can handle the workload while I am away, I can travel, work remotely, and I can generate income when I sleep.

I still focus on growing my companies and the real estate portfolio through partnerships. When I look back to those magazines that my dad used to send me, I never thought they would have pushed me to where I am today. Even though my first home purchase in Johnstown, PA with my VA Loan was overpriced and not a great deal as an investment, I am thankful I made the purchase. It taught me valuable lessons on how to rent out a home and gave me the experience I needed to purchase more units.

After reading this far into the book you may be sitting on the edge of your chair wondering how to get started investing in real estate, but you still fear the possibility of losing money. Let me just say from time to time you will purchase a property that may not be the most amazing deal. I personally write-off bad deals as "tuition" but always keep my eyes strictly focused on my end-goals.

You might be thinking you would get started but don't have the money. If you are just starting out, and you have a housing allowance and/or VA Loan eligibility, I would recommend contacting a real estate agent and start house hacking as soon as possible.

You might be concerned that the market is not prime and the right time to buy was after the 2008 crash. There is an old saying in real estate that says, "the best time to buy was ten years ago, the second-best time is right now." Or my other favorite, "don't wait to buy real estate; buy real estate and wait."

If you are still hesitant but have questions or concerns that you want to be answered, find a community of like-minded investors or reach out to my team or me. Real estate is one of those amazing things that can create a wealth stream, but you must get started. Take action now!

Interview: Nico Gibbs

When did you purchase your first home and how did you find it?

I closed on my first house December 17th of 2013. Less than 6 months after I graduated from the United States Merchant Marine Academy. I found the house through the MLS. At the time I was dating a girl whose mother was a realtor in the small surf town that I grew up in and she would let me look through her account. At the time, I had just graduated from the academy and was living with my parents. Investing has been a part of me since I was 12 years old, which is when I began investing in the stock market. I think this geared my mind a certain way that would not allow me to rent for shelter. To me, that's just throwing money away. I lived at my parents' house as a grown man at 22 years old for 5 months until I finally found the right house.

What was your experience with "house hacking" like?

I rented out a room to a classmate of mine from the Academy. It went well for the most part. For me, simple and seamless is always what works best. I offered him a flat rate for rent that included all utilities. I sold it to him by pointing out that he would never have to worry about a bill or his rent fluctuating. All he had to do was set up a direct deposit into my account once a month. Honestly, this benefited me because I didn't want to split bills every month. That's a headache after a while. Also, because I was bundling everything for him I set the price of what electricity would be every month along with other bills. The only downside is that eventually he would move out into his own house and rent a room out himself. I suppose I taught him too well. The bright side was that by the time he moved out I already had another Academy classmate moving into his room. It was seamless. I will say there are potential issues with renting a room out while you live in the house. "Tragedy of the commons" applies here. When you buy a house it's your baby. You take care of every square inch the best you can. Your renters will not be as passionate about your house. You have to learn how to balance this by only renting to people who will respect your property. This is why I always rent to people I already know. My friends went to the Academy with me and have a natural tendency to be clean and orderly.

Just to bring things full circle it's important to note that my philosophy is that a house is not an investment at all. An investment brings money into your life. Your house will never do that unless you rent out a room. Remember you have a liability when you buy a house until you rent out a room. We can talk about appreciation and tax credits all day but none of those bring cash into your life on a regular basis.

What is/was the best part of "house hacking?"

Just proving your idea right. I come at this from an investor's mindset. Most people buy a house when they have enough cash to put 20% down and cover escrow fees. I have never paid more than 5% down on a house and at 26 I have owned two and looking to buy my third soon. There are two reasons why I don't believe in the 20% rule.

    1) I would rather pay PMI than lock up 20% of my cash. I can make more with the other 15% by buying shares of AT&T on dividend alone then what Private Mortgage Insurance (PMI) will cost me. It makes absolutely no sense from an investor's standpoint to put down 20%. Also, PMI is tax deductible.

    2) If you buy in the right place and at the right time you can have your house appreciate in value enough where that PMI will be taken off. I just did this a month ago with my second house. I bought into a townhouse community that wasn't built yet. I paid $347K for the house. By the time the last one sold at $589K, I called Wells Fargo, who owns my loan. I asked to get rid of PMI, and an appraiser found the value of my equity in my home was greater than 20%. So, I was able to get a new house for 5% down. Only pay PMI for a year and a half and still have my 15% working for me in the stock market.

    Every time I have purchased a house, I have had people tell me that it's not possible. You're going to get spread too thin. It's not sensible. You should put 20% down. I enjoy proving everyone wrong because I am doing what they are too afraid to do.

Have you ever sold or refinanced? How did that work out?

I have never refinanced and unless you bought a house prior to 2010 I wouldn't recommend it.

I sold my first house almost a year ago. It went well. Sold in 40 days, didn't pay capital gains because I lived in it for 2 years, and I was able to write off the realtor expenses. I made $90k on the house and put it straight into the stock market.

Do you plan on buying more properties in the future?

I do, I'm currently looking at a new development going up one block from my current house. It's a little bigger than my house is now at 2300 sq. ft., but it also has a workspace for commercial leasing. I want to phase into commercial real estate as I get older and this development is offering me that smooth transition. Ideally, I live on the top two floors and the first floor will be leased out to someone. I am very excited about this one. Still not sure what my plan is for purchasing the unit, but I'll keep you updated when I decide on my plan of attack.

Do you own a property within an LLC or just in your personal name?

For now, I own just in my name. Mainly because I have never had more than two properties at once. There are many benefits to an S-Corp if you buy multiple properties, but for me, there are more benefits using them as a "primary" and "secondary" home.

I come at all of this from an investors point of view. It's important to me that I make it clear I have only bought in cities that I truly am passionate about and believe are going to grow or hold their value. I also would never buy anything I wouldn't live in. If your aim is to buy a house with the hopes to pay it off one day, negate my advice. It's not for you. On that same note . . . you will move before you pay off your first house, I promise.

Never Sell

The idea of never selling your properties is part of a series of mindset lessons that I go over in our Military Real Estate Investing Academy.

Ask yourself: Would you rather passively earn $10,000 every month starting in your 30s or 40s, or get a lump sum of $1-2 million when you turn 59.5 years of age?

It is not a rule, but rather a suggestion. Of course, there are plenty of reasons someone should or would sell an investment property, and some significant tax strategies that will help. However, if you purchase the properties as good investments and develop your investment strategy with the mindset that you will never sell, it will help you develop a more secure and passive investment portfolio for the long-term.

The greatest fear that real estate investors have is a market crash and a property losing its value. STOP. Passive investors do not invest for appreciation, although that is a fantastic bonus if it occurs. If you concern yourself instead with a property's *rent* potential, and you focus on the cash flow that the rent will produce, you will realize that long-term profitability stems from making a smart purchase. This makes market downturns much more manageable.

"Like the predictability of cold winter storms that show up year after year, market corrections and crashes will continue to rear their ugly heads. We've all suffered losses or know someone who has; maybe it was when the tech bubble burst in the late 1990s, when the stock market plunged in 2001, or when the housing market crashed in 2008. Those kinds of losses can shake you to your core." - Tony Robbins

One of the most important lessons Tony Robbins teaches in his fantastic book, Unshakeable: Your Financial Freedom Playbook, is that after every Winter, there is a Spring and Summer. Whenever a property loses its value due to a market crash, don't let your emotions take over. Don't be scared and sell at a loss. If you are leasing the property and your profit is more than your mortgage payment, why sell? Just wait. If the rent is higher than your mortgage plus expenses, you are *winning*.

Conclusion

As billionaire industrialist Andrew Carnegie once said, "Ninety percent of all millionaires become so through owning real estate. More money has been made in real estate than in all industrial investments combined. The wise young man or wage earner of today invests his money in real estate." This book aims to show you why you can't afford *not* to include real estate investing in your personal financial strategy.

The United States government has provided its military with an incredibly powerful real estate investing tool, the VA Loan. Utilizing it to your advantage as you PCS from duty station to duty station can change the trajectory of your family's legacy and create generational wealth.

Whatever you do along your investing journey, stay focused on producing multiple streams of income. Real estate investing should absolutely be the base-level investment vehicle for all investors. You, the military member, Veteran, spouse, or family member have a distinct advantage.

Action Challenge

Discover what drives you. Sit down with your spouse, friends, family or those closest to you and discuss what gets you excited. What do you love? What would your ideal day look like if you envision it? That is your "why." That is what will keep you up at night and keep you moving forward.

Get educated. There are more resources today than ever before. Spend time reading, listening to podcasts and audiobooks, attend free conferences or join our Military Real Estate Investing Academy to get started. Sometimes just base-level education can be enough to make your dreams come to life. Along the way, you'll undoubtedly network with some great people.

Join a community. Network with positive, like-minded groups and individuals who have similar ambitions, passions, and interests. Active Duty Passive Income has a private social network that could be the help you need to get started on your journey or even take you to the next level (see Resource page).

Use your benefits. As stated in this book, understand how to use your hard-earned benefits as an American service member or veteran. You are among a tiny percentage of people on this earth with these distinct advantages. Why not use them?

Share. Talk to your friends, family, and everyone you can about your new desire to invest in real estate. You will be surprised by how many of them might express interest in joining you or will reveal that they have already started investing in real estate as well!

If you thought the information in this book was valuable, please don't keep it a secret.

Acknowledgements

Adrianne Phillips, Aladino Perez, Allysa Wray, Allyson Kelly, Arabia Littlejon, Brandon Elder, Buddy Rushing, Catherine Livingstone, Chad Payton, Cheyenne Foster, Chris Coker, Cindy Byler, Dan Dwyer, David & Tasha Gwilt, Dustin Nguyen, Erik Clark, Jaime Soto, Jarred Martin, Juan Ramirez, Kateryna Sich, Lauryn Carr, Matthew Cole, Matthew Parker, Mike Chiesl, Military Investor Network, Nataly Sich, Nico Gibbs, Pam Watts, Raquel La Barr, Rod Khleif, Ruth Paik, Ryan Hebron, Scott Hatzung, Sean Taylor, Stephen Anderson, Talia Upchurch, Tyler Gibson, Vasyl Bilokonsky, Wayne Bemet.

Thank you. Your help spreading the word and supporting the ADPI team during the months prior to the launch of this book was invaluable.

ADPI Resources

Active Duty Passive Income (ADPI):
www.activedutypassiveincome.com

Military Real Estate Investing Academy:
https://www.activedutypassiveincome.com/p/military-real-estate-investing-academy

ADPI's Private Social Network, Club and Community:
https://startthespark.activedutypassiveincome.com

ADPI Podcast (iTunes, Buzzsprout, Google Play, etc.)
http://activedutypassiveincome.buzzsprout.com

Made in the USA
Middletown, DE
15 November 2018